MASTERING OPTIONS TRADING

MASTERING OPTIONS TRADING

FIONA STERLING

CONTENTS

CHAPTER 1

Introduction to Options Trading

What is options trading? Welcome to the wild world of options trading. Options are a type of financial product known as a derivative, which, as the word suggests, is derived from another asset, which is usually stock. This means that trading options implies some degree of reference to the assets on which they are based. Like stocks, options are traded through regulated exchanges and have a clearing process for all options orders, allowing traders to take the other side of each trade. We'll get deeper into this with some real-world examples down the road.

Benefits of options trading There are a lot of reasons to trade options. Below are a few examples of the benefits you might experience with them. What we want to emphasize is that they are extremely powerful, and they can be used in just about every financial situation you can imagine. Options let you lock in a price for established periods of time. If stocks go up in value, options can increase your total returns. If stocks go up, the price increases, and when you sell, you can profit. If the stock is the same, but time has passed, the option loses value, and when you buy to close, you profit. This high-level introduction is only meant to provide some context that you will need going forward. There's quite a bit to be learned about options trading, but as you get deeper into the strategies and techniques, much of what is covered here will be delved more deeply into.

What are Options?

Options are a financial tool that enables people to buy and sell assets at a specific price for a predetermined period of time. When you own an option, you can control a significantly larger amount of the underlying asset than if you simply bought a share of the stock outright. And that means you can make a higher profit because of the leverage. When you combine the benefits of options with the fact that you can potentially profit regardless of which way the stock market moves, they become a very powerful part of your trading strategy. The most common assets to be traded through options are stocks, but options are actively traded on all sorts of trading vehicles, including stocks, ETFs, commodities, and even crypto.

Options give investors the right to buy or sell a specific asset at a specific stated price within a specific time frame. When a new trader enters the world of investing, the stock market is usually where they will make their first trade, and that's usually just buying a stock or ETF outright. This is sometimes referred to as a "long position," because you expect the shares to increase in value over time and will make a profit when you sell in the future. And that works fine. Investors who have been at the game for a long time have made lots of money investing in index funds that track companies like Apple and Google.

Benefits of Options Trading

One of the reasons options are such an attractive vehicle to trade is due to the numerous benefits that accompany them. For a retail investor, options' popularity has soared due to the numerous possibilities and opportunities they offer. So, what are some of the top reasons that call options act as such an attractive alternative as a method of investment?

Insurance Policy Many investors that have acquired large amounts of a particular company's stock use put options on a stock of a company to insure their stock against a potential collapse in the underlying. The put option is a security that allows the holder of the option to sell a particular stock at a predetermined price, no matter how low the stock price may drop. Essentially, the purchase of a put option (selling insurance) is a good bet that the company's stock price will fall so low that the put option (insurance) will be a company's parachute into safety. The protective put options contract guarantees the holder protection, regardless of how low the stock price gets.

Cheap McDonald's I don't mean literally cheap fries, rather good companies' stocks become more affordable with using call options. For example, one contract of 100 shares of McDonald's stock will cost you around $14,000. Instead of purchasing the 100 shares of McDonald's at $13,900, you could control the stock for a fraction of that price. If McDonald's stock were to rise from $139 to $145, then the stock would be worth $14,500 and your profit would be around $600.

CHAPTER 2

Basic Options Trading Strategies

One of the best things about trading options is that you don't need to be right about the direction of a security to profit; options give you the right, but not an obligation, to purchase or sell the security. You also can use options to hedge, or protect, other positions that you hold in your portfolio. They offer more versatility than trading stock, with the potential for greater reward and lesser risk. However, since options can be difficult and have a learning curve, it's best to start with the basic strategies. Even retail investors can become comfortable with these trade setups. Here are some basic options trading strategies for beginners.

Long Call: Buying a call option gives you the right to purchase shares at the strike price. It's also called going long. When the stock price goes above the strike price, this is called being in the money. Your call will be worth money, and you can sell the shares for a profit or exercise the call option, buying the shares at the strike price. If the stock price falls below the strike price, your call will be out of the money and worthless at expiration. It will be cheaper to buy the shares in the open market.

Long Put: Buying a put option gives you the right to sell shares at the strike price. This is also called going long. It's a bearish position, as the value of the put will increase if the stock declines in value. If it rises above the strike price at expiration, the put will expire worthless.

Covered Call: To execute the covered call, a trader with a position in an underlying security sells a call option at a strike price regarding that security.

Long Call

The first of the long options is the basic 'long call'. This is generally the starting point for the discussion of options for beginners, and remains the strategy most suitable for traders who are strategizing without regards to valuation or time, or for those looking for profit on larger moves of the underlying. We will get into more complex strategies later, but let's stick to the basics for now.

The 'long call' can be used for both directional and income purposes. Since you have the right to buy stock, you can utilize this option to purchase stock, which you can use as a high-coupon tool. However, for income purposes, covered calls are superior. This is a great strategy to use if you believe that a stock will have a large move upward in value.

Figuring out what stock meets or exceeds these qualifications can be difficult. The importance of this profit potential comes when used with longer time horizons, when potential developments in the underlying could cause large moves. If a stock is entering into a big event such as earnings, it can be a good excitement play to try some long calls, but for the most part, you will want to keep the stock between 35 and 70 and give it at least 6 to 12 months to break even.

Long Put

There are many advanced strategies available that involve entering into multiple option transactions, or in other ways, whether the trader wants to take advantage of maximum options or even without investment or low investment. A long put is a practical strategy. Many traders who use the long put strategy to gain advantage from a decrease in an asset's price will want to invest a price expiration beyond the time decay of the put they are purchasing, or at the very least need the rate on the asset to almost the time of expiration.

Outcomes/Views: The long put may be undertaken as a hedging strategy or as a first step in the use of leverage. For unbreakable riches protection to the downside, then they may desire to use a protective put. One of the downsides of using a long put in either of the two ways explained, though, is that a trader with a small basis will not desire to mix the amount he can be paid investment in the portfolio. The long put is a known method for use in three different portfolio management, speculation, hedging, and earnings. When used for speculation, a long put is a means for investors to anticipate a stable decrease in the price of the underlying stock. They can be the most valuable of the four strategies but are also the most expensive. When used for tailing, a long put can now protect investors in the event of a very fast fall in the stock's price. And finally, when it is used for practicing, the long put can be used by potentially successful investors. Hedgers or investors can purchase puts simply to protect a current stock position. The long put is a no-cost way to do just that.

Covered Call

As a reminder: strategies of this section require high collateral. Moreover, buying power is the same as plain shorting stock. Options cost money to hold, so buying power is more than the actual stock combination. Covered simply means you should own the equity, or already have a long position in the market before selling the call option. When we sell the call, first we make money from receiving a premium. If we get assigned (buy-in), we make a gain in the long position as well, therefore not as rich as owning just the long side. The problem is that if the shares go up a lot, we have a cap on the profit. There are several types of profit and loss we need to key in on this strategy. If we understand what goes into selling a call, we will understand exercising a call option as well. First, we will button down selling a call. Buttons down are a way to make the learned behavior quickly.

What a Naked Put costs (Margin Requirement) + Call Premium Received: This produces a stock price at which, after the call option premium is deducted, this is the price you actually paid for the stock after having sold calls. This is the amount you are overpaying for the stock if it goes to the moon and past your call option. This is the price at which the call you sold is profitable to the buyer. What you think the stock will go above within the time limit of the option.

CHAPTER 3

Advanced Options Trading Strategies

Welcome to the third chapter on advanced options trading strategies. We learned about basic strategies in part 1. In part two, I introduced you to simple directional strategies, collar, and covered writing. I also explained how to identify the right stock option to buy. Spreading is an excellent strategy to use when the investor wants to take advantage of volatility in the market. There are many types of spreads that can be used, but the fundamental goal is the same: to take advantage of short-term movements in the market. Traders who do not regard themselves as professionals use spreads more often than any other approach simply because they do not require precise predictions of market movements.

1. Vertical Call Spreads 2. Vertical Put Spreads 3. Bull Call Spread 4. Bull Put Spread

This series is not targeted at a section of people who may not know much about technical stuff. Remember that using these strategies requires a lot of expertise. As a result, I have assumed that the reader of this book has the following knowledge about stock options and trading.

The reader should be familiar with the procedure of selling stock options. The reader should be proficient in using the best online trading services. This will enable them to figure out how many liquid stocks are dealt in at an online price below $10. Just pick the whole option quotation, but make sure the stock's quoted capitalized size is twice the stock's net cash flow. The reader should be confident in their prediction of a stock's movements. To sell a call option strategy, the reader should know the strike price at which they think the stock will not exceed during the expiration period. If there's anything you don't comprehend, seek the help of a financial professional or a different source. Stock options trading should be regarded as a business rather than a 12:30 event at the racetrack. Ask your brokers a lot of questions. Anyone with a great deal of experience with stock options trading and a good record in trading respects the integrity of the stock market system.

Iron Condor

Once you have learned and managed to execute vertical spreads, straddles, and strangles efficiently, you're ready to explore and understand the potential as well as the risk in advanced options trading. A foundation in options theory and practical application of buying and selling options is required to understand advanced strategies, and iron condors are a great entry point.

If you have been patiently waiting to watch a long-term play where time and theta are key components of both options' pricing, we are dealing with options' implied volatility. If it has been in place and trading sideways long enough to have realized the right part of time decay to price the rest of the months, take your vertical spread to the condor level using the opposite direction if need be. Knowing when it's the best time to roll the chosen option that the stock has not reached yet to give you more credit is also key in this type of trade.

Just like a short straddle requires closely watching the stock momentum (deltas) and the underlying stock because a stock could make a significant move either up or down at any given moment, so could your iron condor. There are many ways to monitor and adjust an iron condor, always be prepared. An iron condor spread is constructed with a unit of puts and a unit of calls from the same expiration month. To lessen the effect of opening the short call vertically and reducing associated margin, the corresponding strikes on the short put and long put are typically $5 apart (stock price between the two strikes depending on time decay) in standard equity options. In ETFs, consider using the $3 wide strikes due to less interest in advanced strategies that would cause more volatility and lower prices.

Butterfly Spread

The butterfly is a complex trading strategy that involves three different options. It can be a very challenging strategy to master and is best left to those with a high-risk tolerance. Trading such complex strategies can have tax implications.

An option is a contract that gives the buyer the right to buy or sell an underlying asset at a specific price at a specified time. An investor can profit from a butterfly spread when they expect the price of the underlying asset to stay the same. The butterfly spread does require an investor to set up a margin account, and it also carries some limited risk along with the limited profit potential. Because you will lose money when you close the position and buy back the sold options if the underlying price does not fall to and through the sold strike price, you have risk the amount of call or put you buy reduced by what you received for selling two. The longer it takes for the underlying to get to the strike you sold, the more you will make, but the longer it takes to break above or below (if you purchased a put) the strike, the more it will cost to take off the two longs you purchased.

In investing, a butterfly spread is a trading strategy that investors use to generate income based on anticipated price movement within a particular range, using multiple calls and puts of the same expiration date. In a butterfly spread, you hold a combination of long and short calls, or long and short puts. This may be a "long butterfly" if you have three long options for one strike price, and two short options at a higher strike price and a lower strike price. Long butterfly spreads use four option contracts with the same expiration but three different strike prices to create a range of prices through which a gain with this strategy can occur. Corrections of value for out-of-the-money options are likely to occur particularly in intervals before expiration dates, making at-the-money and in-the-money options more valuable. This can escalate costs, which could impact your realized profit. Options can expire worthless, meaning you could lose your entire investment in a strategy, like a long put butterfly, up front. Traders might generally avoid carrying risk into earnings or other major announcements.

Straddle and Strangle

In the previous chapter, we discussed the basics of buying calls and selling puts. With the basics of calls and puts clear, we are ready to move into more advanced topics. This chapter will take the first of these advanced topics, discussing combination strategies of calls and puts, i.e., Straddle and Strangle. These strategies are called 'long (buying) volatility' strategies, as ideally we purchase both call options and put options before the strike price goes in-the-money. The impact of volatility on different options trading strategies will be discussed in detail in Chapter 8.

A straddle on the long side is formed by combining a ZCG put option and a ZCG call option. Consequently, a short straddle (combination or strangle) is formed out of Chebyshev's k put and a put option and a call far above or below X, respectively. Many hedgers prefer the straddle over the strangle (it is typically more expensive) because they can have a butterfly structure for free. The butterfly structure is an offsetting gamma position and is generally a more conservative credit trading straddle. Selling or shorting volatility is a concept that is incorporated in the next chapter. The straddle and strangle are unidirectional strategies, i.e., when the investor is expecting a significant price movement in either direction, then only the straddle/strangle is recommended. For example, when a company's results or Fed decisions are going to be announced, etc.

CHAPTER 4

Risk Management in Options Trading

Risk management is key in trading options. To be successful trading any kind of market, traders must be able to understand the risks involved in the various strategies and actively try to protect themselves against those risks. Having a good understanding of the price of the options and the changes in the value of options as the underlying security moves will allow traders to have a better understanding of what they stand to gain and what the risks are. The Greeks, or the changes in option price due to an underlying factor such as price changes, time or volatility, are the primary indication of risk in options trading. In trading, there are no guarantees. There are strategies that can be employed to protect trading capital against some risk, but those strategies will not be successful 100% of the time. The only 100% guarantee against risk is to not trade. Products, like options, that are more predictable, are subject to a higher level of risk assessment. By managing risk and minimizing loss it becomes feasible to manage profit. Instead of being right all the time, trading can be successfully achieved by knowing when to sell when you are wrong.

There are three main strategies that traders must employ to manage the risks in options trading. Learning these strategies will help traders move past "go to jail" and collect on the properties that options can offer. They are: Insuring risks, managing time, and locking in profits. These strategies are often employed without having to watch the market every minute of every day. They can be automated or can be controlled without having to focus on the market incessantly. If you do decide to choose any of the other strategies, these will help minimize losses and make your trading over time more profitable on the whole. If you do not decide to specifically take a high risk, high return strategy in options trading, then that goal will not be accomplished unless you manage trading according to these goals.

Understanding Risk-Reward Ratio

When engaging in any kind of trading, it is very important to consider the risk-reward ratio. This is how to estimate the potential gain or loss that may result from a trade by taking into consideration the potential reward and comparing it to the amount at risk. By doing this, traders can more easily decide if the trade is worth taking in relation to the projected financial outcome. For every trade, it is necessary to figure out how much can possibly be lost and if this worst-case scenario is acceptable. If the worst possible outcome is detrimental to a trader's financial situation, then they might reconsider or reduce the size of the position. Each potential reward should also be weighed against the risk. If the potential reward does not justify the risk exposure, then the trade is not recommended.

The risk-reward ratio can be expressed using either cash accounting or margin accounting. When expressing it in cash accounting, consider the maximum possible loss in cash terms against the maximum possible profit, whereas in margin accounting, consider the maximum possible loss as a percentage of the trading capital against the maximum potential profit as a percentage of trading capital. By using the risk-reward ratio when entering trades, it can give traders a new perspective to see if the risk and potential reward are worthy of trading. If it is not, traders would be advised to start over and look at better opportunities.

Using Stop-Loss Orders

The function of stop-loss orders is essentially the same for both stocks and options: to minimize potential loss and protect the capital remaining in the account. With a wider variety of orders available with stock and stock options, there are many ways to enter a stop-loss order for more specific account management. In addition to determining how much to risk on any option position, it is also important to be able to control risk in an assessment of when to get out of a trade.

What might be most important when adding an option position is also the hardest to understand and execute: when to get out of the trade. Managing a trade is a function of what the market does; a stop-loss order, placed as soon as the trade is entered, helps the trader weather any adverse market activity. Keep from capping the profit on a trade by allowing the stop to be adjusted as the market moves in the trader's favor. The limitations of using a stop-loss order include placing an order with the brokerage firm. Not only do the brokerage fees influence the final outcome, but the trader's firm could have restrictions on where the stop could be placed. If a long time remains until expiration, the trade could be susceptible to loss as a result of being whipsawed when the price comes back up.

CHAPTER 5

Technical Analysis for Options Trading

Technical analysis is the study of financial market action. It involves analyzing market trends, price patterns, and other technical indicators that can help predict the movement of interest rates, currencies, stocks, and commodities. There are two fundamental investors: fundamental traders and technical traders. They each gather, evaluate, and apply different information when making trading decisions.

Technical analysis is the study of the actions of the market itself. At its core, technical analysis is based on the belief that all available information is already priced in the value of an asset. That does not mean that new information will not affect an asset price, but by examining the market data of an asset one can make educated guesses and foresee how and when an asset price will move. This can be applied to different assets like stocks, indexes, commodities, and currencies. Assets can be charted on different timeframes (e.g. 1 minute, 5 minutes, 4 hours, daily) depending on one's trading style and strategy. Different types of charts can be used in technical analysis, such as stock charts and candlestick charts. Technical analysis becomes vital in options trading where the options premium should be ascertained, and this can never be calculated as it is derived from the price action.

During this phase, we will be educating on technical analysis, from basic to advanced level. This technical knowledge will enable you not only to estimate price scenarios, i.e., giving you an idea of the direction an asset may take in the future, but also to assist you in creating options trading strategies, which is very important for generating higher premium.

Support and Resistance Levels

Support and resistance levels are mandatory knowledge for every technical trader. These areas can influence trading decisions, present successful trade opportunities, and reveal likely price turning points. Support and resistance levels help identify pivot points in markets and market sentiment, or the points where a shift in the direction of a trend is possible.

Support occurs when a downward price level is expected to create a pause. It is not expected to reduce the price immediately; rather, it is seen as a floor for the market price. It is also thought of as demand management. Resistance, on the other hand, is the expected ceiling for a market price due to the likelihood of an increase in supply. Resistance levels are generally attributed to investors selling when prices approach this psychological level. A major breakthrough of support or resistance means that the underlying norm has shifted. In other words, the balance in supply and demand has ended, changing the price. Upon breaching a support or resistance level, the terms support and resistance are often turned around since the expected future trajectory has thus altered. By incorporating support and resistance in their decisions, investors can get an idea of what will happen as they can see changes in the supply-demand balance. It will also help traders determine price stop and target settings. Knowing exactly where a stock will change direction can lead to more profitable trades.

Moving Averages

Moving averages are popular and helpful technical indicators in the financial markets. They make the price movements easier to be interpreted in a series of stock market values. The concept of moving averages can be seen from their name as moving, which means averaging of the last "n" observations at each successive node of a series and improving the accuracy levels of the same. Moving averages indicate a trend-following approach and give values by calculating h-day moving averages at each point t.

A moving average is also called a global filter, where each data point in time series is replaced by a moving average of the original series. Moving averages help to eliminate changes in a time series variable since it smoothens the price data. There are various types of averages that can be calculated, but the three main common ones include the simple moving average, the weighted moving average, as well as the exponential moving average. There are two types of moving averages that theoretical or actual returns data is used for this. If the arithmetic returns are used, the moving average is called an arithmetic moving average. Conversely, the application of logarithmic returns will give a geometric moving average.

CHAPTER 6

Fundamental Analysis for Options Trading

In options trading, it is important to pay attention to macroeconomic data and their impact on prices. Macroeconomic studies are important for several reasons and are often referred to as the global fundamental aspects for option traders. Understanding macroeconomics will enhance one's ability to understand the history of their opportunities and, more importantly, it will also enhance one's framework for thinking about potential opportunities at a particular time. In conclusion, the use of macroeconomics will allow option traders to better understand where certain opportunities are within the context of how they are expected to rise or fall due to macroeconomic theory.

A consumer buys goods and services in the market at a price in dollars. Pricing is affected by a number of economic and psychological factors. A growing number of indicators is a relatively accurate predictor of broad-based regional economic activities. It is calculated by some chosen local economic assessments, using periodic reporting, and then calculating the value of the index to get other values. The final figure below the top zero or above is sufficient in the choice of scaling. If it is below a certain figure, it is determined that the economy is being assessed. This suggests that the economy is growing. More weighting is also given to some indicators than the current reading to give a more accurate picture.

Economic Indicators

Economic indicators can affect trading decisions. As a trader, increasing your awareness of the development of economic indicators can help to forewarn of possible changes in the market. Coupled with a basic understanding of how the macroeconomic environment can influence stock prices, these indicators can improve your trading success. Traders take various kinds of information into consideration before trading stocks or options, but analysis usually encompasses two broad areas: technical analysis, in which strategies are based on using stock price data, and fundamental analysis, in which a study of economic, industry, and company data is undertaken. Economically, demand and price risk-share, put to call and dividend yields, option volume, wash trading, dividends versus strike prices, and macroeconomic effects are among the issues that can affect stocks and options. Viewing the stock price in the current market environment must involve the analysis of fundamentals. Although technical analysis has achieved wide acceptance, it is argued by some that past performance has little bearing on the future. However, using just fundamental analysis is now also considered too conservative. Instead, market professionals are increasingly blending both methods.

In terms of economic indicators, when looking at options, it is useful to know the effect on the markets when there are price level changes, expanded production, excess of consumption over production, low interest rates, government borrowing, and inflation coinciding with price declines. Three main indicators are the most closely followed in the US: the unemployment rate, nonfarm wages, and the consumer price index. The US unemployment rate attempts to capture just about all the job market area except for certain categories of people who are not eligible for unemployment insurance benefits or unemployed and not seeking work. The nonfarm payroll report impacts GDP and the stock market. People get hired when business is good. Businesses need to be confident that there's a market for their goods and services before they bring in new workers. Job growth is a major driver behind consumer spending and personal income—spending drives 70 to 75 percent of all economic activity. People work and have money to spend. On the inflation front, the Consumer Price Index (CPI) report released by the Bureau of Labor Statistics (BLS) examines what consumers are paying for a set "market basket" of goods and services. The CPI indicates the rate of inflation for select goods and services. If earnings growth outpaces prices, then consumer spending is expected to keep expanding at a good clip, adding a big buttress to economic growth. Rising wages, just like falling unemployment, are bullish.

CHAPTER 7

Psychology of Trading Options

Trading options has some unique psychological aspects compared to trading stocks. Some of the biggest problems traders face when trading options have to do with whether or not they should get out of a trade, cutting losses when losing, taking profits when winning, following their plan, regret, and revenge. I truly feel that trading options will force you to deal with these more than you are used to if you have been trading stocks.

Trading options can be very frustrating as you can be dead on with your market analysis but find out that the market and time were not on your side. It is the part of trading that most traders have a hard time dealing with and is the main reason so many traders wash out of the business. Emotions and the market, believe me, have no connection. By being aware of your potential for overconfidence, you will be more apt to act on your trading plan. The real art of trading lies in the ability to remain detached from any one trade. The best traders have personal control and knowledge of when to use a tool or strategy. Market theory and the basic tools are the easy part of trading; personal development is the hard part and the part that separates the also-rans. The smart traders work on themselves and do what they are supposed to even if a bad trade comes up. The also-rans keep jumping from one system to the next looking for the right one.

Emotional Control

Many people who think they would want to try options trading have this romanticized notion of traders as courageous people who take big risks to make big money. The truth is that neither courage nor foolishness can aid you in trading, especially options. In fact, emotional control will play a huge part in your decision making. Emotional control is an acquired characteristic that some have and some don't. Emotional control is like fear. They both are inherent emotions. Fear can be controlled, however. Fear, for the trader, is represented in many ways: fear of poverty, working for "the man", failing, looking foolish, and many more.

You can bet that all these fears, even though you deny some of them like "fear of failure" – because you feel immune to the power of that fear – show up in your trading to some degree. In those moments when you are drawing up binary trading scenarios, in prioritizing your trade plan, in selecting advanced trading strategies, in entering a trade that meets all your plan criteria...in fact, the fear that you feel when you lose the amount you gain in a day of work...all of those comprise part of the "fear" that resides in your subconscious. Emotional control is essential to your success as an options trader. Emotional control turns into a close sibling of greed in its many forms. Controlling your emotions around options trading is key to your success as an options trader. In the midst of a market crash, you will have to maintain your wits because panicking could cost you a lot of money. You will also have to occasionally sit through periods of boredom while you wait to be put in play on your options trade.

Your emotions can also lead to you making poor decisions, abandoning your trading plan and doing something stupid.

Cognitive Biases

It is important to know that all your decisions in trading can be influenced by cognitive biases. To overcome cognitive biases, you must educate yourself about them. Biases can be powerful, and they have a steel grip on your judgment, making it easier to believe something wrong. Knowing your cognitive biases can highly optimize your judgment and make it more precise. Overconfidence and automatic thinking are some common biases. This model says that humans are not sort of economic man who maximizes utility any time. Investors have emotions and they trade with emotions, and sometimes they make automatic thinking because of this belief. This makes cognitive biases deep in our root.

One of these cognitive biases is regret, and we traders usually make decisions according to our past regrets. For example, "I will never sell this stock because it has increased so much after I sold it." This is one of the powerful biases that we talked about above. There is a general bias called optimism, which is one of the powerful cognitive biases. Optimism is a belief that your work will be much better in your imagination than in reality. The difference between reality and imagination creates disappointment, which makes you regret and, in turn, makes you automatically think. When you understand the psychology of trading and how it affects our thoughts as emotional beings, you can start to make more rational and objective decisions, whether you trade stocks or options.

CHAPTER 8

Choosing the Right
Options Broker

When selecting an options broker, you should know what to look for to ensure that your foray into options can be fulfilling. Obviously, brokers are the sites through which you will trade options, so it's crucial to make sure that you're at the platform that feels good for you. However, when it comes to just trading, you actually have a lot of options when it comes to brokers. How do you select the one that works for you? Here are some things to search for.

Reputation: What do other people have to say? Look up broker feedback for viewpoints on account management and customer support. Also, find out if brokers operate under larger brokerage services, which may also be rated. Look at registered users to see if they can be trusted. Do they scam their clients? Is it secure to trade stocks through the platform? Tradable Brokers offers brokers for equities trading reviews to show you everything you need to know about selecting the right stock broker.

Setting limits determines the kind of account for options traders. Those who have larger accounts often will have entry to more resources than those with smaller accounts. Ever wonder the difference between a traditional and independent retail or net account? Investors can act separately without anybody investing with most on-line services. Traditional brokerage accounts are immediately managed or can be managed margin accounts. Marginal accounts allow customers to borrow stock to purchase equity. Margin option traders are expected to be approved for margin trading.

Key Considerations

Settling on the appropriate options broker can be a convoluted decision with extensive implications. At the core of the ways to determine the best brokerage service for your needs lies in the fact that every investor or trader is unique with exclusive demands, capacities, and preferences. All of this makes it challenging to flat-out label one options broker as superior to its competitors. These are factors you should take into account when making your decision.

Some details you should consider when searching for a reliable brokerage service include: (1) the quality of the software the service makes accessible; (2) the service's policy concerning what constitutes a tradable asset; and (3) the costs and fees associated with using the service. Challengers are not recommended as brokerages strictly administered in the U.S. are thoroughly scrutinized by numerous independent regulatory organizations, instilling integrity into their operations. A call option differs from a put option in that a put provides a trader with the right to sell a share at a predetermined strike price. An "in-the-money" call option implies a projected value above the current market price, while an ITM put signals an expected share price below that. "At-the-money" options imply forecasted values equal to current shares' values. The difference between ITM and OTM, or "out-of-the-money", options lies in the fact that while the former feature foreseeable results, the latter represent higher risks and higher leverage. This, of course, correlates with calls and puts.

CHAPTER 9

Building a Winning Options Trading Plan

The sign of a professional trader is their commitment to a well-defined and thorough trading plan. Successful traders take the time to define objectives, create trading guidelines, develop and control the tools that work best for them, and rigorously follow their course of action without negative effects in the emerging market environment. Every trader must have a trading plan. This trading plan is the trader's own set of rules. Using the knowledge about good and promising options trading that you can gain from this e-book, any trader can create a trading plan, even if the rules are specifically for options trading. But a good trading plan must include several things, including:

1. Setting Goals: A solid trading plan begins with the identification of general and specific objectives. All objectives should balance the feasibility of gaining a certain percentage of profit per trade with the wisdom of doing so.

2. Trading Journal: Make a trading journal. This simple thing can provide a place to refer to when you are not sure about the rules you have created and applied in the trade, so that these rules can be enforced.

3. Risk Management Plan: A good goal in terms of risk for active returns is to have the money that goes into trading split. One third goes into a retirement account, one third can be used for medium to long-term investments (about 3-7 months), and one third is for active trading. For me, this is fantastic.

Setting Goals and Objectives

Before venturing into what readers probably deemed the "real" materials on options trading, it is essential to remind them to use a structured approach. A common misconception about trading is that novice traders have to start by learning about the right products and strategies before they can come up with trading plans. This is not the case because options trading profit and probabilities in general are subjective to trading plans. As such, it is important to start with the path of least resistance - setting clear goals and objectives.

The specifics of goals and objectives setting will depend on individual considerations of money, time, psychology, etc. For convenience, it is rational to boil goals and objectives down to numerical terms. This can seem unnatural yet serves a purpose. Using numbers help decide whether trading objectives are realistic and thereby setting rates of return (ROR) that quantitatively balances and humor an appreciation of the risk undertaken in trading compared to others. It also helps individuals to segregate trading goals from the constraints justice defined. In effect, we put aside the operating capital we have dedicated to trading into an account with which we chalk out a step-by-step plan. It also calls for scalability. Balance flexibility with specificity by diversifying trading objectives across shorter- and longer-term time horizon. Draw upon one's personality, aspirations, competence and trading environment. In choosing a longer-term objective, take into account soda trading know-how and anticipate the conceptual trade-off between size of edge and number of trading ideas to be embarked on during the course of fulfilling the longer-term objective. Importantly, write it down and be ready to refer to it. A list of dos and don'ts as options trader, including responses to stress, are presented that will enable anyone to plan for the long term, take breaks from trading and move one step closer to success and financial freedom.

Creating a Trading Journal

Trading Journal Basics: This series would be incomplete without a section on creating a trading journal. A trading journal is a log or a record that a trader keeps in order to track their trading performance. It provides traders with valuable data related to their trading activity. The journal is the place where traders reflect on their trades and analyze their performance. Based on this analysis, traders are able to improve their trading strategies, refine their techniques, and avoid making the same mistakes over and over again.

What Tools Should You Use? At the most basic level, all you need is a good old-fashioned notebook or a basic word processing program. Many traders prefer Microsoft Excel because of the many built-in functions and mathematical formulas. We think Excel is a great product as well. If you are not familiar with Excel, we have included a section in the Master Study Guide for you. We have designed an easy-to-use worksheet that anyone can use. This Excel worksheet has all of the columns needed to capture all of the information that a trader would need to record. Note: This tutorial is based entirely on the information that is recorded on the tracking sheet. We do have some clients that get into extensive software programs that track every market and option trade that they do. For the beginner and the experienced trader that does only a few credit spreads per month, we find the tracking sheet to be just fine. The following are some examples of key information that you could track.

CHAPTER 10

Executing Options Trades

Exiting or entering an options trade is as simple as either entering a new order or closing a previously opened position. Again, the brunt of the action is actually in setting up the profitable plan before options begin to move. For the most part, options will be executed in the exact same way as stock itself. The main difference lies in choosing the strategy, the right option, and choosing the right ending in order to deal with closing out other positions. The decision of whether to enter a market order or a limit order to close the option will rely on various factors. Calling for specific types of sell orders can depend on how liquid the option is, how fast you'd like to enter and exit, and how briskly the options move up or down.

In a market order for liquid options, this will close out the trade at the currently available market price. More often than not, this method is a very efficient way to get into or out of the position when options are moving steadily, with no unusual price leaps. The lot will be sold at the price that is currently quoted; barring any unusual circumstances you will sell the lot as soon as possible when the order is received. A market order for the purchase of options generally moves quite well. At the very most you are leaving a nickel on the table as you wait for the order to be returned. You can usually close the existing position as soon as it is transmitted. Are you long for the near money or even the in the money options? A fair market price bid should be let go of the bid amount.

Market Orders vs. Limit Orders

A market order is an order to buy or sell a stock at the current market price. A market order guarantees that the trade will be executed but does not guarantee the price of the trade. Hence, market orders are tools of the impatient trader, immediate traders, and the novice given that professional traders use less risky systems. When placing a market order, investors ask their brokers to buy or sell immediately at the best price. Generally, stock exchanges match buyers with sellers according to price, and so when investors use a market order, they give up the chance to improve the price. The order is given in a form like "I want to buy or sell this stock at the best price." A buyer will get the stock at a market order price higher than or equal to the limit price. A seller will sell at a market order price lower than or equal to her limit price. Further, when a market order is used, the trader can bank on getting her stocks anytime she wants. Very vital, the trader can either wait for stocks to come to her or make stocks come to her immediately. There is no limit to when stocks can be bought or sold.

A limit order is an order to buy or sell a stock if and only if the desired price is reached. Thus, while a market order guarantees that an investor will buy or sell a given number of shares, a limit order guarantees only that the investor's orders will be fulfilled at a given price. A buy or sell limit order specifies the highest bid or lowest ask price at which a trade will take place. Conversely, when a trader places a limit order, market players wait for her to execute prices. A trader thus gives a directive to buy or sell only when stocks enter a specified range. It thus means that limit orders limit buyers from buying when prices are high as well as limiting sellers from selling when prices are low. Consequently, the results of implemented trades are not guaranteed.

CHAPTER 11

Monitoring and Adjusting Options Positions

There are some pretty good arguments for why you may want to adjust your options positions. Equity prices and index levels are fairly volatile. As prices change, so do trading opportunities. Over time, the price of an option can change fairly dramatically, even as the value of the underlying benefits. Volatility can fluctuate, and as it does, the pricing of options responds as well. The passage of time is a concern – as an option gets closer to expiration, there isn't as good a chance that economic conditions will change favorably.

Of course, this is what makes trading options so appealing to many – options are dynamic, and our perspective changes as their pricing does. If trading opportunities are different now than they were when a position was initiated, it may make sense to make a change. We also may elect to make a change based on whether we think an option's price is too high (or too low) based on our projections about the share price, implied volatility or other variables. Because no two portfolios are alike, the decision to make an adjustment is based at least in part on your overall objectives for the options (or stock) positions you may have. If you aren't currently using profit and loss targets and assessing the likelihood of differing outcomes, it may be better for you to evaluate potential changes from the outset to be in alignment with your trading plan, rather than checking in once a day to see what our present premium levels are. As we noted at the outset, trading options necessitates not just investment analysis, but also portfolio management. Options trading itself is dynamic – and using a combination of strategies only increases the need to actively monitor and manage positions, as any one adjustment will impact not only a single option contract, but a number of others that may be part of a larger strategy.

Rolling Positions

Shadowing is an important retirement strategy. When a leap is expiring in-the-money or a leap has become vested, it's time to roll your position. This section contains roll ideas for long leaps that are in-the-money, at-the-money, and out-of-the-money, and for short in-the-money leaps due to be called.

Stocks and leaps don't always cooperate or move the way we want them to. Taking no action is not managing your position. Rolling up and forward can increase our potential profits and allow us to continue using options to pay for leap buys. Rolling a short option out can turn a losing position into a winning one. It can mean the difference between a winning leap and the early execution of a leap because it's in-the-money or about to expire. It can lock in profits before they disappear.

Find strategies for the following movement: Stocks moving from bear runs to bull runs or any combination of such moves. Strategies for the following stocks: stocks moving from bull runs or a combo of bull/boring runs to bear runs or a combo of boring/bear runs. Strategies for stocks and leaps in different modes: for instance, a stock in a bull run while its leaps in a boring or bear run. It's time to roll a position when a leap is expiring in-the-money. If we like the stock's prospects, we can roll up and out. Our gains will be much better if we roll up and out. Rolling puts the position farther out in time allowing us to ride out the next downturn.

Rolling puts the position farther out in time, and gives the stock a chance to rebound and leap again. The first half of the move was completed by BRLI, moving from a bull run to a boring run. Following this, we roll our in-the-money leaps, preparing for the next half of the stock's move. In practice, we've rolled LEAPS positions before stock movements. Our analysis showed that they would come in handy. Shrewd options traders can quickly and effectively adjust and/or extend positions in a way that's beneficial to both losses and profits. We lean more towards advanced strategies in which the roll transaction doesn't necessarily increase inevitable losses.

Closing Positions

The trading process doesn't end with the opening sale of options contracts. You must also learn when to exit options positions. Closing out your options position means taking the equal but opposite action of your original position. So, if you sold to open a position, you may repurchase the same options contract. Or if you purchased to open a trade, you may now, in turn, sell to close your position. When considering which options positions to liquidate, consider the following factors: portfolio objectives, options strategy, and profit targets. By taking the following into account for each particular position, you may evaluate whether to let your profit run or secure a favorable gain from the position.

The credit spread seller is not required to close out the short options in the strategy. It may be more favorable for the trader to simply wait while the options expire out-of-the-money. This allows the strike to become worthless, offering the maximum gain. Adjust the order for the offsetting leg strategy to be similar to the closing order for naked options. However, recognize that the investor still holds short options. Enter a buy-to-close order at the inner market for the short position. If the spread is wide and the market is moving fast, consider pricing only based off the short position. Sell an option currently held long in the spread. If a broker realizes the long options position is profitable, they may elect to sell the long options.

Alternatively, any options that are out-of-the-money can expire not worthless and take at least a small amount of profit. Investors must avoid in-the-money options, as they will quickly need to be offset. In looking through the reviews, someone also asked why with the Calendar strategy they are charging a credit or why with the debit Condor they are looking at the total cost. These people have clearly not done their homework. They keep trying to argue with the writer of this book. The reason is... it must be subtracted out of the final gain or loss. This way, the investor/speculator can tell if they did well. Say they receive $2 and pay $7 for a Condor. That means they lost $5 on the trade and should place that in their trading log. With the Calendar, they have received $3.5 but need to list that cost. So, it's essentially a short trade on the back months. This should be increased by the cost of the calendar. If they paid $4 to make $3.5, it's only a cost to them because they also receive money from selling the front month.

CHAPTER 12

Tax Implications of Options Trading

Finally, when discussing the financial details tied to options trading, it is important to give consideration to the tax implications. Trading options and engaging in options trading strategies represent taxable activities according to the IRS and can have a number of potential tax ramifications. When implementing such strategies, it may not only be important to consider the individual strategy's total transaction cost but also the potential impact of taxes.

In general, a basic understanding of the IRS's treatment of trading activity may involve the following points. First, receipts or profits generated from the purchase and sale of options are collected directly through the proceeds from premiums earned or paid. The purchase or sale of an option can generate either a short-term capital gain/loss or long-term capital gain/loss. Traders are taxed at the short-term capital gains rate if the option is kept open for less than a year or the long-term rate if the option is open for a year or longer. Upon the closing of the option, those gains/losses are realized and the individual will then be required to pay those taxes. Always remember that when dealing with legal entities such as corporations or partnerships or retirement accounts, the tax rate and treatment can differ from that of individuals because different tax laws apply to different entities. Therefore, an investor should speak to his/her tax adviser before conducting any trading activities to obtain this clear understanding for the specific details of his/her trading.

Capital Gains Tax

Three theories underpin the feeling many option traders have that options are taxed differently than other trading instruments: 1) the lack of an actual sale, 2) the combination of gains and losses, and 3) the drawn-out timing. Under federal law, capital gains result from the sale of an asset, and a net gain is reached after taking out the cost of that asset. Essentially, if we sell at a gain, long-term or short-term, we are taxed on that gain.

This feels very straightforward when we are talking about selling the shares of a stock, but when the shares of the stock we are talking about are actually an options contract, it becomes more complicated. This same approach can be taken when identifying short-term capital gains from options. The sale of options results in either a known gain or loss, and the purchase of an option results in either of those outcomes as well, yet in reverse. With straddles and strangles, it can seem that a gain is realized simply by buying the strangle or straddle at one value and selling it higher, but this potential gain can be wholly eaten up by the premium outlay with the next set of transactions. Instead of having unlimited losses upward or downward as with futures and margin trading, many option trades have a known profit before entering the trade. While additional profits can be made with options, the capital gains tax bite has to happen early before the gains are entirely eaten up in trading frictions. Knowing this can help with tax planning.

CHAPTER 13

Case Studies in Options Trading

If you have ever struggled with thinking about how to manage a trade or apply a strategy, these case studies are written to help you gain that insight. We are going to cover trades that are winning, trades that are losing, trades that have three different market conditions, and strategies that are applicable to different market conditions. Every chapter in this book revolves around a specific subject; each case study presented in that chapter will have letters attached to them. Then, every time the case study is referred to, a page number will follow, to help you locate the situation.

These case studies (or "examples") are exactly what the title implies: examples. Every case study included in this book is a real-life scenario, straight from the lead author's trading account. These trades are taken directly from the author's personal spreadsheets so that every entry, exit, and price will be reviewed. The goal of each case study will be to help you learn from someone who has actually been in the trades. When trading options, strategy is 90 percent of the battle. Every process from "step one" to "exit" should be clearly outlined in your trading plan. As you go through these case studies, please think about your own plan. If you cannot make an answer to a question about a position, it means you need to improve your plan. The following pages should help you build and refine that plan.

Real-life Examples

In this section of the book, several real-life case studies are examined to describe the application of options trading strategies and techniques in a variety of markets, ranging from bull to bear, choppy to neutral. We also consider the gamut of external factors that can negatively or positively affect the underlying stock when evaluating the performance of the trades.

Those experienced in trading aggressively can sometimes diversify into less risky cash-building techniques such as covered calls, or the mom-and-pop retail traders can implement speculative trades in periods of increasing volatility. Some are bullish while others are bearish. Thus, in this section, the purpose is to assist a variety of individuals doing a variety of things at any given time who might benefit from practical experience to ascertain what might work the best for them in the wild world of options trading and to see what happened in real life with techniques others in a variety of situations have used for such financial vehicles. In some examples, there is a set-up; it will have a trigger; others will not have anything due to the nature of the strategy applied. From recent picks calling for a rapid rise, to gaining leverage on the S&P documented through various vertical spreads, through simple bull spreads or put ratios, to outright long positions, to utilizing protective puts on a low-priced stock showing signs of continuing strength, this book covers a lot of territory in what can be applied.

CHAPTER 14

The Future of Options Trading

E merging trends Ever since the markets bottomed out and have remained strong since 2008, there has been an explosion in the understanding and use of derivatives, and in particular, options. Prior to that time, there was a huge movement by options exchanges to promote options trading, especially in the retail market. Educated, well-capitalized individuals dominated options trading. At the pits, it was not unusual to see positions of thousands and even millions of options contracts held by one or only a few people. Nasdaq and exchanges wanted that retail volume. While there are still discounts out there, many firms are only for the high net worth, hedge funds, etc. The options trading community also became "big." Multi-million- and billion-dollar profits powered the industry to new heights utilizing options to develop new trades and to further its own purposes.

That means those pits would have been ghost towns except for their clients who want to hedge exposure using real assets. The hide- and hunters only have the ability to enter their orders through a broker who executes them electronically with liquidity providers. Almost gone are the floor brokers who walk around the pits shouting orders. Not completely, though. The CBOE still has a small, remaining floor presence. Options trading and volume for proprietary trading, and due to the spreads available, as a market-maker, has collapsed. Once hot, the S&P 500 options 'pencil' market has seen volume collapse by 70% in a year. It is important to understand why most options are traded by proprietary trading firms.

Emerging Trends

The world of options trading is constantly changing. Since options exchanges began operations in the 1970s, the opportunities available to options contracts have increased and changed many times. It is possible that some major shifts and alterations may take place in the options landscape in the years to come. We would like to identify items which are perceived to be speculative or controversial. The readers should keep in mind that we are not in the business of prophesying the future. Just because a particular trend is judged most probable does not mean that it is guaranteed to occur. Readers will therefore wish to view each trend described as one possible future. Also, readers should be on the lookout for the emergence of other developments which are not discussed in this section.

A number of dynamic forces are shaping the world of options trading today. Some of these patterns have been in existence for years. For example, computer technology has been advancing for a long time; one would have a hard time arguing that this element of the modern era is a "trend" as of 2023. Meanwhile, some other key developments have only become significant in the last two or three years. The following trends and forces may or may not come to pass in the future. Some may continue into next year, while others will not be relevant next year. The marketplace works in strange ways. Some of these forces are generally supportive of growth in the world of options. Other forces can be very adverse to the growth of options trading.